sundance publishing

LITTLE RED
READERS

Talent Night at School

**PETER SLOAN &
SHERYL SLOAN**

Illustrated by Virginia Barrett

Last night was talent night at school.
All our parents came to watch us perform.

Some children formed a band.
They played some music.
All the parents clapped loudly.

Some children put on a play.
They acted out a story.
All the parents clapped loudly.

4

Some children sang.
They sang songs from the radio.
All the parents clapped loudly.

Some children danced.
They leaped around the stage.
All the parents clapped loudly.

Some children told jokes.
They made everyone laugh.
All the parents clapped loudly.

My friends and I were magicians.
We made a toy rabbit disappear.
All the parents clapped loudly.